HOME RADIO

Luke Roberts

Published 2021 by the87press
The 87 Press LTD
87 Stonecot Hill
Sutton
Surrey
SM3 9HJ
www.the87press.co.uk

Cover: Veronika Pausova, 'It Holds Itself' (detail), oil on canvas, 18"x15" Courtesy the artist and Bradley Ertaskiran Gallery © 2021

ISBN: 978-1-8380698-8-9

To relieve the nagging suspicion that we were being buried alive, we often went out in the morning for coffee.

MUSA MCKIM

Acknowledgements:

Many of these poems first appeared in the chapbooks *Left Helicon* (Equipage, 2014); *Keep All Your Friends* (Materials, 2014); *Pocket Song* (Visitors, 2016); *Headphones* (Visitors, 2018), *Rosa* (Distance No Object, 2019) and *Inhalers* (Equipage, 2020). Thanks to Rod Mengham and to David Grundy and Lisa Jeschke.

Some were also published in the following magazines: *Artichoke*; *Botch*; *Cumulus*; *Datableed*; *Erotoplasty*; *Hi Zero*; *The Hythe*; *The International Leg and Cutlery Preview*; *Mote*; *para·text*; *Snow*; *Splinter*; *SplitLevel*; *This Corner*; and *Yule Log*. Thanks to the editors and everyone involved.

For Amy Tobin

Contents

[POEM]

Imagine a theory of narrative
and another and another and another.
Imagine a theory of turquoise.
It exists.
Night all glossy I could stage this.
I could just stage this and stage this.
And when the light hits the seagulls
just so
it makes all of them look just like geese.
It's good to make sweet generalizations.
Like light specific to winter
will always graze over your bones.
Beautiful talents
come back through the front part
bronze bark in the daylight
catching the wind.
I could just stage this and stage this.
And at exactly 3.15pm this time of year
all the trees in the park just glow.
Is the poem empowering or disempowering
I ask my students.
I've started to think this
this is the best stupid question
as arbitrary and precise as anything.
You can do this any time of the day.
Sun's out in South London
and city gifts drift across the river

arriving like geese
too early and late.
And history's citrus descending.
Just say it it sounds good.
History's citrus descending
beginning with grapefruit
and ending with lime.
This is narrative.
And this is the theory of the narrative.
Late   Beach   Boys
world with a bite taken out of it.
Beautiful talents moving slowly.
At 4pm I think about my life.
I saw you, you know this, I saw you.
Ready to go in search of virtue
hauling all the winter work in stupid shapes
and I could save this.
I could just save this and save this.
Someone walks into the room
and opens a book
and says *you* isn't a signal
it's order and love
it's the forecast the forecast the forecast.
And shame is often beautiful.
Vague speakable daylight.
Vague speakable day.

MATING SEASON IS OVER

Melancholy default the footgrips
   dismantled an abacus with my elbow,
cats running circuits round a post
   high above the legible beads. First I cleaned
the floor, then I gave it up. The wall socket
   in its seductive composure writes the day's
calibration of practical ethics. The tip
   of fingers running in a circuit
on a cruise ship, there are two, then
   two more, then climbing undressed
the disturbance has an outline, links
   the good head cottons on itself. I was
conceived in summer, time spent building
   a frame of good tension for the wrapped table
how like myself looking to comprehend
   cause and personal affect. The breeze runs
through and the taste is sweet and it remains,
   false change come from the pocket willing
you must know all the hands without counting.

It was your hand worked to capacity, switched on
  the margins brought from sleeping tones
to know where you are. The politics continues
  to press with accountable cross-links, needs
no praise from the quarters, a list of demands
  writ on the morning's surface and curving
across the crown. The desk-fan joins the desk-lamp
  fraying the remaining descant, beating out
the settlement in intervals they descend
  from the roof, cross the square and river.
There is a stretch of glass reflects the body
  and the motion bound along the arm
it knows the fling is limitless, drawn
  up the features of a rose garden opening
you leave the contents to be determined.
  It is the lasting day before the next month
carries its childless bowl back and forth,
  the shift glances against your shoulder, bare
like the lovers, poised in love's suspense.

IT HAPPENS

Engels, the beautiful walrus, his hangover
    in England, where we learnt slowly
from the home, leaning our faces
        to the snow,
            surrounded by wildlife and orphans.

In this poem I will imitate my lover,
    nesting in the library
        and make her voice appear for company
beside me or maybe slightly up in front.
It will feel like stealing. It feels like the man said
and I said this morning:
                in the family the man is the bourgeois
etc, with a wave of my hand
and dropping my forehead to take the air out
    but the other part is more important.

I want to go to a Jewish butcher,
    be greeted like a friend,
and buy a boiling fowl, but I don't know
what part of town to go to.

        I should be applying for a job, but
this morning I read about Eleanor Marx
    who killed herself, but lived a street
or two away from here, with the sea
in her ear and I'm distracted. Her translation

of *Bovary* gets trashed on Amazon. This
is the voice of Veronica, hurt but unsurpassed,
and E. P. Thompson's melancholic line
tips me back in my chair cracks me up:

Everyone else was always impossible.

Then I imitate Neruda from memory:

Tired of being a man,
I walked past the barbershop
and the sound of electric razors
and laughing, the walnut, the coats
and the coughs, I was anxious.
I was sad. In the bookshops, I hung
my head of sadness in the pages
of the books. The pose brought my eyes
to the season, empty with citrus,
and locked in the orchards of crisis.
I wanted to grow my ferocious beard
in defiance of the government,
who I hate, every day, as I hate
the police, and their clothing,
and their shields.
I no longer want to buy or sell
a thing.
And my prison face.

But he was a rapist in his autobiography,
        and in his real life presumably,
with his green knife and his profession
of honesty, like Helene Demuth and her son
        running a household where the writing starts.

I did this all day, and the day got slightly longer.
My abandoned poem is in the notes you hear
for real in full:

To watch employment in real time
    my companion Hercules in molasses
the grass is so white and sheltering.

        The colour of lapwing.
        The scheme of anything.

Spring in the only world there is,
    a child of regular size.

C. AND THE FAMILY

What's the light work doing right now for emphasis,
the screen shaking its head, and how did it learn to do that?
Other bold questions sound off and resist the corners
of touching. All the places I live, all the buildings and recipients
go back and renew our permits, fresh for a clear run headed off.
In the incident book for recording the climb there are casualties:
maybe forgot how to do it, clung to the wrong mast
or the sliding clamp to check what everyone's watching.
One of our number felt burning. There are three faces at least
and you touch them. Maybe when they look away I'm still
speaking, asking the motionless day to show me its ballot.
By the law of average achievement like the temperature it drops
straw over the conduct, holding items up in front to cover
the breakage. My behaviour is completely exemplary.

Once you tell the coast your intentions, the real focus remains
on the interior. There are returns and you greet them determined,
wary of straying too far from the base. This is my calculated
walk-on voice in character, stepping back to the corner
of working. Get into the key and push: I hate the float
shedding layers of recovery, growing cool by exposure they grow
drowsy. How many buildings on our street how many street-lights?
For sabotage to be effective requires targets, each Dutch sapling
sold-on, air-born, like the tips of beautiful wages on the seafront,
speckled with the wrong type of sea-life. No-one's past-time,
nobody likes that, twelve canoes in the only colours canoes come in,
and each of their riders standing up, waving a white flag, opting
for security and exchanging an earplug for a share of the profits.
Such threats intensify in line with aging, flatten out.

Each terminal blank so far is a hand, but I only have two hands,
taking up a seat in the stalls too many. Can't ever be enough
contact hours in this condition, unremarked in this order,
standing apart from bad figures of complaint. I wake up blinking
in a familiar province, read our Commissar on the question
of laundry. The arrangement of old implements in new quarters
or halves: making animal noises, we examine ourselves for defects,
go to the brim and be full with a voice on loud
and unafraid. I have probably been in a thousand buildings,
but am open to dispute. You look like everybody's cousin,
brilliant in orange, the bright day original and fast. It took seven
hours for me to say so, returning to the beach and the joins
of tender display. This is my best voice added to the current
from scratch, the vocal record of customs and citizen objects.

For every evening unaffordable and the four categories
of housework, one in each corner I know how to dust. The phones
multiply on campus, make mock of the central aspiration:
nobody gets their clothes any cleaner that way, but the donations
stack up on the old model, to say nothing of reproductive labour.
I only gave blood once but I liked it, despite the faint sad
feeling afterwards. You can see my arms better than I can, see my
legs in the structure of a joke, also from the past but much nearer,
stationary and attached to my torso. The next person you call,
you give them a lesson on anatomy, distorted on loudspeaker
and wait for applause. Despite this, and the sky elsewhere burning,
eyes raised to the floor of the floor above, like the hint of a garden
behind either password or user-name, bound to a script, taking
slices around an appetite deferred for the scene of homecoming.

Went to the dispensary anyway and folded, holding a cup, smiling awkward in the fashion of a man. The lack of white goods is not a tax, just a hidden cost, depending on which end you speak from. Ana does the morning shift, and at lunch-time Marcia takes over. The boss comes and locks up at night, applying a diminutive to all the machines, his handful of necessary time gives you a flavour. I, lacking strict accuracy, start spilling the powder. What could you possibly know about this in the Alps, a three-in-one general purpose agent grated all over a toothbrush. Wearing my clothes at the public swimming pool and whistling the best pleasure with no answer, and the clouds curling like milk, what lengths to go to, how ground down in sustaining garments. You are a cousin with no false movements, adopting the breeze as it lifts our skirts in a sign of good nature.

Dilute the soap to stretch it. 24 hours before the bi-annual reunion, immersed in sexual detective stories to cotton on, who do I fill in for? My handwriting is almost illegible. There are five months lost in the details, heads above water continuity, facing a catch and acting like poachers. The gulls wake me up, timed to the arrival of the workers at the site. Behind us the solids call up and appear to the side, fresh and shaking out the shower, with a new understudy to embrace. It is not a clear day, but you secure clarity in every room to enter. A tour de force loomed over the crowd when the building stopped burning down but not yet and still nowhere to slide to. You have two weeks of socks, half that in the winter. What you do when you walk around, collecting an impression to offer and store: tell them I'm still here, okay, everyone up late clenching their fists.

SUDDEN PROGRESS

Two years of sunburn distinct
but on the same surface clouded to account for,
counting out the facts and what to fix on.
At first the verbs were feeling like a belt, down
goes the prediction, forgets my name. The same
thing happens and you bounce. The outside
world was doing its thing, and you, anyway,
were walking around, occasionally neutral,
occasionally scared.
            I had to quit the ballet for my own good,
my feet, my figure. A womb with a broken ankle
in the middle, suspended and disgraceful.
It stopped hurting so much, it joined the other
points in a different run, from the side of the day
to its ending. My role in the sexual economy
is negligible, I said, as the parts came together
embarrassed. It was the same airport, so-so,
waving face-down in the coast, then over
to a district of floating. Part of my family wasn't
born here, part of my family grew up here.
I could have said 'negotiable', like a boat
or an obstacle, but I heard her talk of sailing
and turned down. I turned later to the recent
shape of friends. Say hi to the animals for me,
give them part of my love at least, close the window
when you go to try to sleep. And fortune last of all
goes wildly along, flecked with disbelief, a flake
of pleasure strengthened against the profit ceased.
There are bitter things you can put in your mouth,

sharp things, organisational choices, but I will never
be one of them. At this the ground clears his throat,
corrects your estimation.
Did you encounter any difficulties?
Did you leave everything as you found it? Yes and No
are adequate children, holding hands. Their heads
are too warm to stay here.

AGITPROP (AN ODE)

Kids dressed as kids dressed as wizards
        beats individual chorus deployment, plurals,
the crane operator on his lunch break
tied to a chair:
        free assembly at the summer camp,
            dancing in a long line, filmed for posterity
                hazing styles redrawn
                    by a fair hand
                        declaring emergency
always thinking on the future dysfunctional
        the dry heave on the dry run sensational
            but what's not error if not valuable to retain
                the division of the division
                    and I can't get bored with sums and games
because the crowd is looking awkward.
        The poem is about disappearance,
            missing persons
                an entertainment accompanied
by artificial flavours, perfume,
        blackberry and bay, a licensed masque,
            which takes you to a slump of sugar basis
                replaced by clear citation,
                                argument in form
which clutches and lets go in time to music
            wants to be alone in the black-walled house,
                handing your instruments to the fleet,
                    banned from string duty
                        you get the tone wrong
cutting everyone's throat in Paris
            holding up the ribbons blissful
                casual bluff the steps and presentation
                    and it blows

or breezes picking up,
unties him in tireless admiration,
for diversions of a pleasant kind.
What I was doing was stretching out but cramped
heavy tracking unsweetened necessary velcro.
I don't think efficient disposal will help you
be more attentive, combing through the scans
amused by fjords, spring water
for rousing sunlit persons,
running through dry grass its operations weaken.
A bad analogy, many bad analogies, paintings
in the garden watching through a window, a kitchen,
the regular hours, the increasing span,
playing house
arrest now
that I live on a street with police.
The granary is special because community
giddy with criticism, hands you
a scythe and a hacksaw, instructs you to sever
the legs. The job falls to you because your ancestors,
patrilineal, were experts in the field
of prosthetics. But expertise is not genetic,
I got no science and nowhere to sit.
The idiocy of rural life comes home,
peasants in the Winter Palace crapping in the vases,
degrading beautiful things. Gorky loved
good hygiene, the best for everyone
and it's Spring. And now that it's Spring
Pindar, getting ancient on my own ass optimistic
how quaint. Some poems you don't mention
the slaves, biting a fat tongue
pushed on the teeth when you're angry,
stalemate by the fire recounting visions,
wading through the cherubs at the feast of Venus,

fainting at the hot dogs, making
a safety announcement
in another tongue entirely.
If it was a biblical dream of weightloss you were having
you were wrong, taken by surprise
in our own backyards
by a squirrel,
young, stuck, and desperate,
pissing in mid-air.
I put the squirrel in a box,
throw it in the road, posing
for a photo, ashamed and hungry,
the thin song issued from the standard channels.
Tourists will always be with us in praising a house
intruding on problems of devotion
in theory you welcome attention.
Reluctant to honour the movement of blood,
domestic commitments on the world stage
put away the spade inside my skeleton.
You move in the quarter made eroded
relaxed the rules for locking arms allows for sidesteps,
jumping square-to-square, and no
wet clothes or sea-salt there
to greet you. It is perfect seeing often,
often mistaken,
but rare to lose the body when the floated heart
is resting, all its pretty actions revealed
the slightest terms:
wildness in the middle of depression,
survival and disaster, aversion
to risk as exposure to knowledge
prefers the early work on the highbeam,
the learning curve restricted
and alighting, no fingernails left to cut.

But catharsis as a measure is no fun,
and you can't run with phallic charms,
that's why Hermes had sandals
decked with wings.
The marble pavement closes,
he is enter'd his radiant roof
entirely radiant, so we say
thank you to Jupiter, put the radar in the child
watch him grow. I grow around it, evasive,
strategically so,
pinning my hopes to my own tail
which wags in independence,
staging posts, vehicles, metabolism, the aching ritual
not the nearest or most crucial understood
to want corrected forecasts.
Insufficiently insurrectionary,
on a work placement for three years paid for
by the state, not to be blamed
nor changed is anything in two
different cities
but not so different so I send my apologies.
The poet dreams of totality,
but Pasolini sided with the police
and you nearly lost a finger in the fleece
when it was time to get to grips with disappointment,
become didactic, slipping in and out of uniform
as it suits.
Excellent coat,
excellent new deodorant,
excellent boots.
It was the Gospel According to Matthew
but you were thinking of Medea at the rally
for the teachers caught by hailstones
generation of tender vipers

and Herakles outlive us all,
running through market square with the left wing of capital.
The weight of a talent,
a life of anonymity, loose as an adult lost
waiting for analysis.
The prize is wasted,
too small to share the hinge
I rest my case on.
This is what you get for playing dumb,
a whole generation of writers playing dead,
fixing up their brands and flawless assets
in advance, switching larynxes at leisure
quoting Pasolini and the opening chapters
of The Class Struggle in Ancient Greece.
And the police get over-time
and they get to wear protective clothing.
And the peasants over time
begin to dream of protective clothing.
You get used to being arranged,
the discipline,
wrestling with the weather deadpan
bringing in the corn
ignoring the failures, falling in love
with self-criticism.
When they look the same you feel safe.
When they leave the room you feel safe.
The work is hard:
Patty Hearst married her bodyguard
and who can blame her,
April 1979, an episcopal ceremony at a Naval base,
weeping for her children
on the cover of Italian Vogue,
sporting the look that makes spring
and the whole mythical history of kidnapping

look easy.
Successful images exist on several planes at once
goodnight three seven zero
reflecting the fantasies of many.
Take me to the bodies if they're dead
describing the flaws in our music
to the despised, abandoned the nets
never to come down the halted chase.
You're so
inconsistent, siding with the poems,
putting the lean on up in arms without criteria,
whimsical, thrilled to be raw and devastated,
washed with news and frisked.
The friendly machine,
the medicine, coasting unwaged
forgets to save a part for such returns,
famous, slightly older in the lasting sound
of what was done in names of doubles,
cleaning up the glitches strewn
between the homes of acted fiction's custody.
The story just runs and runs,
an electrical fire in two great arcs
high above the Indian Ocean,
Comrade Bala out on bail
in the mild climate,
face turned to the sun, and the wind
in our sails to guide the waves
with true love I survey the wreckage,
hating to end in climax,
360° of coverage disguised
to hide the faces, saving
the special characters
who wait for moments like this,
a pause in turmoil

a break in the action
so you can say goodbye, or else
ditch through the exits
gathering all the actors to your chest,
happy now dispensed with glee defective.
But there were gestures of my own
and you imagine me,
stepping over bodies without comment,
waiting for the airlift and the cranes
all dipped, drawing on reserves of grief
reserved for such occasions.
The brief is continue to live,
and my daughter's name was Olive
in the singular.
The secret poem
meets the wheels in stereo
fully grown, telling stories
of our absence
told to you and you alone.

A POEM FOR DIPLOMATS

I wanted to tell you
brisk like an appetite
for what's an appetite but telling
yours is later, always later, always there.
Run the sensitivity into light, skip back
a screwed up lesson in your hand
of love's rarity, blushed and covering
the change when it covers like relief.
Fleet and destiny be my theme, for as long
as there are themes fulfilling the requirements
gather early visits on the ground
be my guide and gatherer, leaving behind
the half-chewed anxieties about placement.
Are you strong?
Do you consider the stray daytime
in context?
Night is dedicated to attrition and discount
rhymed the long season of arrival
when I bowed my head I had to stay still.
And we were rid of the darts
I was chafing on fluency
costumed in romance
stretched to fit the certain outcomes
of uncertain states and legal status,
how we blur the powers when they're mounting
and there are no defenders
too literate for my good.
This means pick up
and the chorus says use
pretending to furnace where my feature belongs.

Is the middle always vacant
                                        or is it too crowded
all the loud and quiet elements, effortless elements
      to meet
                  after meeting so often.
                                        And why don't you like that
when the water slaps you
                                        cheek to cheek
I whisper every dirty joke about clarity I know?
                                              I don't know any.
I don't know how any
                        one unit could measure & furnish
what the details do, what the prospect does, the best change
fulfilment of purpose.
                    This is a love poem for diplomats lost.
I want a beautiful desk facing your desk
                                  and the ending of daylight.
                              The plans would be blue, the flowers
from the block and the new heart's figures arranged.
      Want to bypass and be in the water
                            when it's frozen to the ankles
and the hips.
                  These are not men will support you.
The founders are buried in something other than snow.

It is summer.

It is summer.

And everyone knows.

A POEM FOR EARLY RISERS

If desire is constitutional
you mean constitutive
weaving on a rickety loom
to illustrate
how such phrases could save us
the waking's less brittle
and pleasing to the touch
like sap or gum
or other things sticky like wit.
This is a little song
and obvious,
writ in bed in August
August
still still still
the sickly skies still total and white
too long to see through
too still to heat my own self
self-demonstrative in two.

A POEM FOR OTHER PEOPLE

Marx he called the Greeks
the normal children of humanity
rude health who don't get a stammer
improving my syntax,
but you all knew that.
I couldn't tell who was in the house—
but someone was moving around
and there *was* a house
of formal portrait
followed by complaint.
Dear cherubs—
I was not made to be an announcer
pushed to the brink of a stage
when there is no announcement
and no stage.
The shelf falls down
the paint begins to boil
and the fixtures start to lisp.
This is a hymn to Venus indecisive
are you serious.
Are you serious, are you placid, are you warm.
Are you your hymn to Venus really
and in the sequence of land and sea
your favourite is the Caspian—
for the salt spray seals the windows shut
and there's a patch of oil
on an upper platform

where the turn turns into a twist.
When I was a boy I was a shrill moralist,
you were also. When I was addressing
the wheeling constellations
it was sleepless. The whole world was sleeping
except me.

POCKET SONG

i.

For harmony, dust
I’ve been testing my weight
dust was my body’s accomplice.
Dust was lettered
and I was its litter
the sweet world was ending
and I was its song.

ii.

Devotional
tight-lipped
fricative

wherever my legs
would take me

twists in the distance
the boring sublime

in the city sincerity flew

iii.

I snuck into the city.
I admired its buildings and drills.
I lived on the sixth floor
      daily descended
              and nightly returning
collected the matter at hand.
The heat would enter my left arm
       and leave through my right
but my sweat was constant and even.

iv.

I snuck into the city
chokes close to the road
supply and demand
demanding.
I've been standing alone
and October is closing
contact with water
contact with air.
Give me your best arm for steering
let me take it
and change it
the exchange rate
over emotional.

The heat leaves through my clothing.
The cranes hint and I'm hinting.
With my hands in my pockets.
With my hands in the air.

v.

In the evening
overwinter
indispensable

I plundered the fruitflies
gave up the gnats

made solemn my glorious
company

I tested the features
I knew how to move

Europe the sun and my hangover

vi.

Europe the sun and my hangover
twists in the distance
in the city sincerity flew.
Glamorous summer
where are you running
now the shelf is held up
by our heads?
Stronger than thought
more humid than thinking
the bed turns over the ceiling.
Glamorous summer
braced for discredit
quick-willed and quick-witted
these were our feelings
this was our rumour
run down instead of taken
for surprise.

vii.

It's hard to distinguish
joy from aggression

with the moon so low
on the horizon.

Like a tough cousin
roughing up the carpet

I tidy the damage
with my eyes on the floor.

It's hard to extinguish
the light in the street

where to look
when you're told
to stop looking

viii.

The scale flips out
warms up and I'm failing

like a feeling reduced
by conversion to steam.

The heat gets everywhere
twins me with sailors

This was my data inhaling

ix.

This was my data emotional.

Talking body and finance and method.

Talking joy and aggression
            how we came in the season
the city's sincerity
                        is what I report:

Kids on bikes
            on Ontario Road
                        midnight outside
the Century.

            We love the golden sun
beyond its apex.

    We love the urgent sun
            in its emergency.

x.

What night is it
in the city
where you are
and am I visited.

Is it the same
wherever you go

wherever you go
escaping.

I can see Mercury
signal to his brothers
crying on the night
resisting its takes.

I can see summer
resting on the city

now sacrifice excitement
now show me how it's done.

xi.

Show me how it's night
in the city,
where we go
without guides
for completion.
How will I recognise
the others,
how will you find me
if we abandon
the station
the necessary materials
of elation?
Our mathematics
our philosophy
our instruments.
Simple lessons
simple asthma
simple bridge.

xii.

The same but we meant
the equivalent.

We meant the theme
as a constant velocity.

Difficult friends,
we were given a task.

These are emblems
for everyone's use.

The sun on my head
is indifferent.

Inhaling the data
in sweet dedication.

This stretch of my body
my functioning summer.

xiii.

It was never sweet.
  Think of the street
    the danger of the street
as a surface.
    Did you ever get fixed
on description,
      on carving on song,
the theme and its cousins
    repeating?
That’s how you catch it
    sky heavy and definite
that’s how you catch it
    repeating.

xiv.

Now it's morning
        and I'm listening
                and it's morning.

Amy says Simone Weil says

        Art has no immediate future
        because all art is collective
        and there is no more collective life.

It's a trick of the light
    and I'm not used to this light
            after the brilliant compromises
of night.
    And it's morning and I'm listening
being held in the voice,
        and the world isn't ending
    and I'm morning and you're night
            and it's coming

            love unbroken by the sun

HEADPHONES (I)

8/1

Let's say winter loyalty
on the slow down
royal
with all the gorgeous trash
how we miss the unrest
we can't make

14/1

Just one form among many
or is it one form flung heavy
breaks when you touch it
when you were calling your life off
or the parts of your life
something must rhyme with
faking surprise
night fucks up the building
still stunned by the summer
high and faint and mesmerized

9/2

Evening purple tulips
this time loss
does it *for* me

when a poet dies
green tips empty
green tips open

I get off at floor zero
I'm broken

read this one back
in slow motion

17/2

January,
                    and the time for lament
one of those winters
                    where everyone gets sick
I mean everyone
                                gets tired
rewinding the muscles
                                  collapse into collage
when the ideas are so thin
                    and the poems take so long
                               you'd think
we'd be fitter
                    with all of these stairs
all this heavy lifting
                                    heart-to-heart

no heavy breathing no stars
just the birds and the swings
crows and parakeets,
a big golden pigeon
big endless January
taking forever
twisting my ankle
& chasing you out,
remember?
I don't know,
but I'm sure the politics
is making me sick
fixing a lemsip
yellow tulips by the sink
limescale cracks like the arctic
and the attic somewhere else
fills with water
returning from a voyage
days of crystal
nothing twisted in the tactics
of the capital
no snow no medals no grievance
no good tracks to cover
now anything other
than total surprise
would leave us all raw
and vulnerable.
I feel exactly like this,
six o'clock
February 17th 2017
exactly like this
whatever you want
to call it.

19/2

A sweet punk dog,
everyone looks sad
we say hello
sit down
stand up on two legs
beneath the glitter
I was older
than the day before
the day before &
maybe it's dangerous
to spin the fixtures like that
through the window blue lights
came on as I was talking
this chalk tastes bitter
my work wasn't knowledge
good boy
good boy
good boy

24/2

Oh but gossip was our sometimes glue. Oh but gossip
screws things up, upsets our sense of balance. But maybe
we were standing on one leg, on a chair, hand to ear,
leaning out to catch the breeze of brilliant news.
You can choose to be astute in stepping down.
Awkward circle, awkward silence, how you soften
and retract, how you often understand the catches
much too late, and in the wrong voice, in the wrong
climate, anything you find is worth keeping.
I love the loss of quality. I love the screens.
Ribbons trail me in my sleep and tie my context's
indiscretion to the sound of bolting horses.
Like jumping up and down to test the branches.
Like a lesson with the title second chances.

1/3

My time got different
                        scenarios
I was its gradient
                        lost
but not losing——

There were sometimes long months
            lost weeks
                        to be tough but open
and not so
            overthrown by feeling

——Oh but banished
and from our own house
I mean this in figures
trash to the ankles
looking for treasure

19/3

The next thing was to wing it
fucking constantly
                    back-to-back
either side of the Ides
of March—
                    our ears
were always burning
& our pockets smoked
looking for the story
and the stars.
          Well yes,
                    I saw it—
I was always seeing it
something like bad luck
turned into a weapon
two men sleeping
          in the park.

25/3

And we were nothing but dutiful,
punished by art.

1/4

I couldn't keep up with the reports.
I started lying. Anytime anyone
asked me for comments, I said sure.
I said sure, it is the duty of poets
to know what year it is. But some days
and some weeks we weren't certain.
So I said sure, it is the duty of poets
to be uncertain, really only poetry
discloses our condition.
                                        But this was ridiculous.
So I said, sure, only comedy is perfect,
I mean real comedy, the whole set
falling down, accidents of any kind,
real hurt, slipping into a river
                                                            like a language
                                    being eaten
                                                            by a bear.
                                        Is this the dereliction
we were scared of? Some little speech
about abrasion? How will you measure
real pain?
    We used to meet people from the future,
now it's the future,
                    and we can slow down decorum,
drop the front and say whatever rhymes
well enough, well sometimes I've been
full of shit and I've continued, tactile,
all this, and my heart.

The question continues to be *why*?
This part is called confession
without a subject.   Now you,
you climb up on my back now
and tell me what you see.
These tests are literal.
I'm failing you all.

1/5

'And it is unworthy of a Marxist, in general, to present the history of literature as though people are ruining each other.' (*Viktor Shklovsky*)

'In the early period of my career I was distinctly able to levitate. Peer pressure against virtuosity stopped me.' *(Trisha Brown)*

14/5

Everyone's from everywhere else
place names and slang
in a rectangle
on the square—
I meet you where sleep goes
instead of sleeping
I picture a tidal island
and everyone goes
from there to here
drinking beer on the street
and I was unfair
selfish for experience
shared out in twos
counting months out on knuckles
fuck experience
fuck a big monument
I'm a good traveller
I'll travel anywhere

15/5

For a while forgot
what country I was in
couldn't recognise people,
their faces, my language.
Couldn't recognise language.
It's the bonus of decades,
not to get lost, hostage
to love of technology.

You like the impersonal
surface. Sometimes forget
I have friends, I'm alive
and this is nothing
            and everything.
I was diluted by warmth
by walking myself
to exhaustion. Someone
in the flats gets buzzed.
Or someone outside,
in my earshot, offset
by birds and cars.

30/5

Lime into maple variations,
it's our signal: only one poem
opens any time. Write it
with your right hand,
listen to the neighbours
and the night.
Condense and distress.
In the night there's no
feeling, only movement.
The world tastes like metal.
I can't taste it.
It opens and it closes.
Nothing touching nothing.
The voices are waiting.
You're wasting the night.

31/5

What's not my forte beaten
by the gap between the poem
and the time of its arrival:
the last day of the month
whose name is stricken
from the record and the weather
is green and bright and fragile.
What's not in the poem exists
inside and occupies my time,
it crowds the room with message
and survival, how the clouds
just bloom on the horizon
refusing to answer, refusing to say
a thing to pass the buck
and fuck debate and fuck debating
what I wish for can't be written down
can't be spoken, can't be said aloud.

1/6

Something elated or latent in the detail,
I'm exhausted but the details stack
and now that my public
voice has come back it doesn't matter
that the motive twists an arm
distracted patience.
Smoke doesn't rise it twists,
and time in Paris changes if you listen
listen careful, listen brave.
It's noon and outside LSE
we're reading poems to the workers
out on strike.
We're not on strike.
            I don't have poems
for this, read Vallejo in English
with the workers doing movement,
that's my day   that's my whole day,
no guilt and soon it's June the second
and time changes in the strike,
even if the movement shows that
you're the one who's miming,
put my body in it, put my poem
temporary on the line.

2/6

Desires of no location breaking ranks,
voices in the park and through the trees
just coat the evening but it's really night
and time for real companions
not the franchise waiting in the wings
but is that us? it isn't clear who'll bank
the total concept in the unforgiving
night, but fuck it, I was wrong:
                    the trick is rust for everyone
swerving to exist, but fuck it twisting
with the bitter part of best inventions
not yet possible to grasp
                    I have the better answers
                    you have the better questions
                    even the plants need attention

JOY SPARKLED IN ALL THEIR EYES

Right now the days are too fragile to move
high and scraping the calendar
too much scrutiny bruised us on tape.
But don't be confused by joy, afraid of error:
I have been sublime and seen the other
late in the decade
stripped of agility, learning to turn
we have our own words for these things,
movements, announcements, and news.
Sometimes you stay awake all night with friends
and strangers. Sometimes it's good news,
or at least the news feels good
even ending in stalemate feels good to be right
but don't be consumed by the shapes.
I mean the graphs and the colours.
I mean the seats and the day still to come.
The title of this poem is a joke about Milton,
because in the line right after he talks about voting.
Really it's a joke about us.
I had some lines by other people written down.
The artist Ida Applebroog says,
this is not a kite / this is a 1% glimmer of light.
Ignore the numbers in your own time.
The artist Ida Applebroog also says,
more mysteriously,
a golden screw with no message
why?
I say that she said it, she painted.
Draw the inside of your water-damaged body.
Draw your hand with your hand and start counting.

The point is this is also a message.
We were golden threads running through the city,
through the city half-invisible
and when we said light it was light
the big grey kind of light, light grey
no source just even and strong
no origin
tired of admiring the sirens
combining pure form
right when what we needed was analysis.
I mean this with no expertise.
If you weren't there it's like a letter.
We needed something to celebrate
because it's better to be bold and capacious
to gloat and laugh with grace and half-humility
late in the decade with no expertise
but something social and feeling
all we did was knock doors and hype.
When I'm in a stairwell I like to whoop and clap.
I like the pure form of the echo.
I like to be doubled and tripled.
I'd like to be the twelve minor prophets
but the days are too fragile
or the days are too volatile and tough
and I'm nowhere near volatile enough.
My favourite character in Jonah and the Whale
is the Whale.
My favourite character in Jonah and the Whale
is God.
My favourite character in Jonah and the Whale
is the plankton,
is the 40 million plankton

the Whale must have eaten alongside Jonah
every day. Or twice a day, rising to the surface
at night, caught by golden threads.
This is a poem about biomass and voting.
This is a poem about the twelve minor prophets,
Milton, the artist Ida Applebroog, the Labour Party,
the first eleven days of the month of June, millions
of edible plankton.
The game of favourites is lesser identity
and sometimes you just have to choose.
There's no joy in plankton or whales, rising
to the surface at night and spending the days
avoiding the prophets with nothing to chew.
Sometimes knocking on doors
wakes up people on the night shift.
This is bad prophecy, bad timing.
No-one needs to be woken up.
Jonah was asleep in the whale, the whale
was asleep, the plankton slept in shifts,
my voice was sore
my heart was over-excited
my biomass was incalculable
my life was one of indulgence, pure
in the grey light of morning
we were neither inside nor outside the whale.
E.P. Thompson says another name for the beast
of history is experience; even the swindles
have something to teach.
E.P. Thompson is forty million plankton
furiously swimming to catch you.
It was 2017,
our ribbons were trailing in the wind

and our fires made the smoke more bearable.
It was a poem completely falling apart
because the content and experience
was serious
but I reverted to the past tense
deep in the habit of lamentation
it was serious but not solemn
like the minor prophets, eaten by whales
marooned on the shores of Iraq.
Sometimes a terrible metaphor
turns up at your house when you're sleeping.
Sometimes you're the metaphor,
waiting for the government to fall apart
wearing my short-sleeved summer shirt
because it's summer
near enough midnight
and it's sweet williams on the table
pink and green and white
near enough blank
72% of young people
turned out to vote in the election
and what I did in the poem was
I moved the flowers indoors.

FLYER

There are people too embarrassed
to confess the wreckage with adequate gravity.
I am one of those
people who when surrounded by patents,
or orange flowers on the table,
white table attached to the wall and the floor
reaches for my own throat
with my own hands nervous
because the years made me nervous
or I'm pretending, touching my mouth,
pressing my thumb against my finger's index
I'm in no danger. It's just me
and the de-humidifier. It's just me,
the de-humidifier, and the humidity.
There are cities where heat is collaborative.
I am one of those
cities built in the wrong place,
inadequate lungs, beautiful trees,
the river and streetlights punch out the dark
and two great plane trees, four of them
sixteen, twelve I've never counted
but they fill the park with fibres,
I don't mind. They avoid me
when I'm in the house, windows open
open windows most of summer
dry the walls out
and the plants all die from under-tending,
soft rituals and fakes,
crystals on the shelf to please the visitors
catch the light,
be salient and numeral
treat the air like my brother

watch the campaigns falter and restart.
All we need now is an animal,
trained to fetch us our papers and materials.
But I don't feel now attached so much
to information.   I don't feel now
so informed or so important,
                                        oh my
informers, how much of it
even the best things and lasting tastes
shaping up and saying it great
is fooling ourselves and everyone else
happy to be talking and standing?
I lived through all this and none of it.
The political break.   It looks like
nothing, because it won't stay still
and won't arrange itself
in details worth recording.
So what's the difference between syntax and image?
Questions are hard to pull off.
You have an empty body,
equal in size to the building,
equal in size to the air.
Planes fly through you.
Planes fly through you and nothing comes out.
I am one of those planes,
failing to take off and failing to land
and outside the day is beginning to behave
as badly as ever.
The men in fatigues make you tired.
You don't see them but you feel them,
like a dead leg or broken ankle
it's easy to be laconic and staccato,

to stumble for comfort
doing the routine lit from below.
But the country is covered in blood.
The country is covered in blood
and always is. That's what it means.
There is a language real enough to know this
happens.   I am that language,
part of it luminous
afraid and covered in sweat.
What's the biggest number you can think of?
Numbers are hard to pull off.
I don't think about numbers,
I can feel them
running in my chest and swimming upwards
swimming upstream, building cabins in hiding
a whole house of nothing but exits.
You look up,
                        and I look up too
what else is there?
I didn't make this decision
caught slipping for everyone's destiny
call and response
soft rituals of representation.
I am one of those rituals,
        easy and overwhelming
sleepless running in the wreckage every day
civic value
too embarrassed to sing
because most of the distance is walking
or throwing keys from a window
or catching keys thrown from a window
thrown from so high up the risks are too great

but we're greater,
lying on the roof to catch the sunlight
ears open to danger and change
slow and reassuring
that's why your syntax is plain
and the images are clearer and clearing.
I am one of those clearings,
coughing up trees and questions.
I wanted to hear myself answer the door,
give myself a lesson, tell myself I wouldn't vote
for someone like me, because the record of my party
is disgraceful.
Whatever building I was in when I wrote this
doesn't matter
                    drawing breath
learning when to draw breath
and what to do with it.
You might need it.
Someone might need it.
Keep it because someone might need it.
Nothing's easy.
Light cuts the building in half for half the day,
and the wires expose the dust,
white paint, the work, the workers
the conditions for light and for breathing.
What's the difference?
What's the opposite of lying flat,
mouthing victory to the ground
giving shape to a feeling with gravity?
Nothing but surface, nothing but
difference, the thinnest of things
is what's holding you up.

EPITHALAMION

for David and Gizem

There are three cities I can think of,
each more elegant than the last.
The first city is covered in pollen,
and in the long grass the poets
hide their songs and blush.
We come to it.
I came here to learn about love
and how to be brave
and what will save you from a life
of nothing but adjustment
to the way things are
to how the clouds already
and all the animals and buildings
and the language and the shadows
and the noise and poison
is ready to transform.
The evening star is everything
you love, collective life and struggle
like the bud emerging into light
extends the day and makes the laurels
for to crown your sleeping heads.
The second city looks like dust
and passports in the summer.
We come to it.
I have never been the summer
but I love the way a visitor
comes to find the songs and sings
of love and insurrection, brave
and fair and beautiful. You know
the heart, you know the heart

of a poet before the law
is everything you hope for,
that's why the wish is public
and we love you each together.
This is the gate and entrance,
made of names, desire, and truth.
And if it's sweet it's also fire,
makes the bitter bearable
and teaches you to taste until
your teeth begin to hurt
and all the dirt beneath your feet
receives you with the freshness
you deserve.
We believe that everything is always
changing, and what we celebrate
is change. What to term it now,
how to live it, and the story of the city
is left for you to tell, each and several
hearts historic and believable.
Bells in the poem
fireworks in the poem
peacocks in the poem
dolphins in the poem
parades in the poem
banners in the poem
children dancing in the poem
to the side extravagant.
The city beyond description
is where we live, dust and pollen,
whose name is mystery and beloved
and what you are is given daylight
and what you need is given night

and what you leave behind is sweet
impressions, full of joy and fortune,
ready to begin.

HEADPHONES (II)

23/7

You know as well as I do:
breakfast with oracles
          dinner with wolves
I have no fingers left.
I know my style is outdated,
twice bitten and shyly admiring
my thefts. I know when I peak
and I crash. The wolf
                    in oracle's clothing
told me so, sharpening his teeth
on my song.
        And if it sounds like allegory
it's allegory, but the costumes
and lines are all me.
        This time the flowers are red
and perfect,
          and if they sway in the breeze
they sway in the breeze.
    And if the question's hey Luke
hey poet
          my answer gets carried away.
What are you if anger's deleted?
Where will you bury your head?
          What you know is what
I know and what I know is this:
                    the sky mistakes our gift
for taking turns, it burns
for three days straight.
          On the first day the oracle
extracted our teeth. Goodbye teeth.

On the second day our pockets
        grew fat with honey and song.
On the third day the wolf grew tired,
opened his jaw, relaxing his hold
on our throats.
        On the morning of the fourth
we took off our costumes
and nervously took to the streets.
The social function of art.
English surrealism.
The rural avant-garde.
I keep trying to count on my hands,
but the sky is honey decoy
        sleep gives up no secret
and sometimes I have nothing
to say.
        Understand that this was my answer:
        really there's only one story,
        I just tell it in various ways.

24/7

What are poets? I said, running headlong into the gravel.

What are poets for? you replied, leaning against a pine tree.

I know this game.

A hand descends from a cloud.

The world scoops us like ice-cream.

You don't get treats for getting it wrong.

30/7

Morning & the plants
it's time to drink
                    I think
the autumn will be
turbulent.
                    I think
it's best to be quick
good to keep dry

bury our grain

you do the same

6/8

The adults outnumber the kids
except when it flips.
It's August the sixth, warm, Sunday
a little overcast and so
Jamaican Independence in the park
above the rocks, the steps
the dinosaurs beside the lake
behind the sphinx above the tower—

we stayed out an hour too long,
the whole thing unfinished
and nobody's business
                              baby universe
I was trying for fictitious
but the facts press me hard

in the middle of the maze
there's a maze

7/8

This week peach stones everywhere,
          wearing money in a sling—
had it, lost it
          and I refuse to live through
the crisis in America
                    but that doesn't get us
very far.
               Solemn options deluxe
and our colour scheme is orange
                                   & dusk—
you keep yourself surprised
          custom for no-one
                    littered my feet
for heat and forever
        for bridges very close
                    what language is it
you ought to be talking.

9/8

In a pedalo
on the Danube
a pain in my side—

Obscure again.

A kind of damage.

A kind of storage.

For me to make
a story with

For me to make
some song

11/8

Never cold enough—
        drinks on planes
I count eleven lights
   and stop counting.
What you learn is
skills for something like
survival
only at the expense
of everything out the window—
and it's expensive
     the skills aren't skills
who needs another masterpiece
of self-incrimination
    I was two drinks deep and flying
beside the Mediterranean
        in the dark made silent
by movable air.
   I clenched all my muscles
including my jaw
getting weaker in fact
by the hour.

17/9

Lemon & asparagus
& butter
            carpel tunnel
Sunday morning
        & everyone still awake.
Southwark Council & Lendlease
                    are criminals.
How corrupt does a city
                    have to be?
How much method
        where I'm going
                    will I need?
Plastic flapping in the breeze
                    like a sail
surrenders everything
   for this or any other season,
                    ringed by smoke
and bits of language
                    on the ruins.
Southwark Council and Lendlease
                    are criminals.
Say it on fake dunes in Burgess Park
                    & learn the names.

                    White sails means money
                            & a big blue crane

18/9

What need the arctic people love starlight.
Okay. I will go so far with you.
I will go so far with you & no further.
The retreat on water burns my hands.
These are the extremes, if you want it.
Just a little hot and cold to pass the time.

20/9

Satire boils out of the ground
I scoop down to taste it
& it tastes faint
and good—
the sky peach with sepia halo
I love it
I love the word *epoch*
but can't fit it
escaping
to my frame

22/9

Absurdism is over. Then the storms
came and I was thirsty
like a fever
but predictable and mild.
No-one can cancel
a category,
no-one can junk
a condition.
But the first major phase
for my generation
was slapstick and pranks,
low-grade,
the West,
men doing minor harm
to each other's bodies
and their own.
But OK. Today I watched a teenager
doing long jumps on concrete
dusting his fingers with chalk.
Oh man,
these are idle thoughts
my balance is off
I was never an athlete
and athletics is over
it's just terminal weather
state legislation
totally static
long jumps on concrete
how you handle the air.

17/10

Damage twin you are my best twin
night faultless and nearly faithful
you're my voice or
part of my voice
next to no good next to no good
OK with fate
OK with that
bandaged in language
like a bird.
You're my best twin,
night constant and thorough
night fateless and fake
you're my best twin
standing in the place
of desire,
tested in the place
of love's allowance
worn away with damage
& thinking
of the heart's best thing
OK with fire
OK with that
with all the tender
all the friends
I haven't seen
defiantly in years
OK with years
you're my best twin
next to nothing
but the sound

of being tested
by the day as it recovers
and the night begins to turn
and the traces
of attachment
start to burn.

25/10

I keep thinking it's Easter

do you keep thinking so
too?
The drops are for comfort,
I've been writing them
for years.
It's easy to forget
how everyone
feels
King of Tuesday
& the night
it sounds confused
but really it's clear
and the air was divided
like this:

oh crystal
tell me what will happen
survive the night

but it's the day
where danger is
& the damage
in us too.

light doesn't
escape

doesn't flicker

oh I'm a child still
still need protection

little light come here

tell me true

tell me what we're going
to do

1/11

Fruit in the fields
ice in the freezer
dreamy & going to waste—
you crush it with your teeth
to hide the taste
in films from
1987
but the year
it doesn't matter
is the year
forgot, forget
I lost my book
and went looking
in the bank
and in the segments
of the city
piece together
all my steps
and who I stepped with
what I did
and why I did it—
all the best defences
all fledgling and sun
all spilling my hours
to bring you closer
too hot in the head
too flushed by sky
for sure
for sure
for sure

I know living is a fringe
                    event just
                                        ask the dead
and newborns
                    my opinion
                                        cheap and green
and tired of frowning
                    like a tour guide
                                        out into the traffic
filigree
                    & dovetail
                                        & filigree
& dovetail
                    like a satellite
                                        taking my phone
and scraping the freezer
                    cracked with ice
                                        with apricots and forests
calling me home
                    but only if I'm needed
                                        now and now for real
and even so
                    the tone begins to clear—
                                        deep grasp of *things*
sweet sleeping
                    hidden in the back
                                        of your lover's head
let's say in 1987
                    but the year
                                        it doesn't matter
now I'm talking of parent
                    but everyone listen
                                        listen clap each other's

hands
          across the table
                            ask for water
when it's warm
              across the office
                            and outside evening
is shaking his fist
              and work turns off
                              turns off
turns off
              the nothing news
                            like nothing lights
and sugar paper
              sugar lights
                            to bring you closer
simple stuff
              living & dying
                            what you're doing and why
and for who
              in this location
                            understood by no-one
more-or-less
              burnt caramel
                            on the roof of my mouth
but sweet and wasteful
              the root of my trouble
                            just ragged and effortless.

7/11

I take the short cut
behind the kitchens
where the bosses park their cars
& the guys take cigarette breaks

I know I'm good

from my side I can see this,
bumped out
loved & troubled

I know I'm good

I know this little stretch
where the birds live
& the pink
always crush & green

who cares for fine distinctions

languid ambassadors

big yellow light

lights for everyone

2/12

Thick in the middle of the year
and nowhere else. Will you be as wide
as a warehouse, soft as straw,
shaking your head with the others?
To my brothers to my sisters
nothing less. Will you ride out
in daylight's disaster, ready to praise
and be praised? I wanted to tell you
raising my paper
nothing less than this:
                                        I'm listening
and I'm waiting for the faintest,
ready to faint and come to gasping
at the brutal little tokens,
harsh taste
                                December
make a joke and make another
                        make a noise and feeling
bitter little lyric
go easy

AERIAL TACTICS

Out of AZ

Woke up,
snow sounds like someone typing
gentle and brooding complaint.
Sometimes the whole world
feels like reverses.
But who are you
to say so and stay warm anyway
and give your warnings
in the gold and green light
pink sunset last night
the whole frightened scene
tilted so the light
slides off and hurts us?
I wanted to describe the silver dome
the three children trying to climb it
the man in denims running
and the shadows of the birds
but the liar's trade keeps knocking
at my window.
The men from poetry want to see
my papers
and the strike dissolves us in silence.
I've been in a bad mood all year,
hating my desk
heavy melancholy splendour
the year of the dog
running to keep up.
Who will keep the strays alive
if we're silent?
Who will whistle when I tilt

and disappear?
Ice covers the edge of the playground,
with the pines all pining
                                        trees acting like trees
spring buckles at the prospect of conflict.

This year spring's so fickle I renounce it.

What's the universe?
                                And am I naïve inside of it?
The handful of snow slides out
of the body,
                                is it ready?
And why's the world like a baby?
                                        Or a flock of babies
smelling like babies?

Where did everybody go?

                                What happens to the snow?

Which of my friends will flap
like a flag and melt like the coat
of a dove?
                                My time is afloat
and immaculate.
My time is the news on a timer,
                                switched for the whole world
primed for the struggle of spring.
The traffic in steel tariffs,
                                the real unblemished chorus.
Tilt so the light keeps on hurting.

It's the element,
porcelain, honey
the houses and numbers
I gave up on.
I never think of Italy
or the crowd of babies
finding their way in the labyrinth, glass,
ringed by woods and splendour.
We were shadows, smoke,
gold marathon blankets
perfect in the arms of a stranger.
Someone at work just had a baby
on my birthday back in March.
I tell the father
it makes me feel like I'll live longer
weird logic
which I still want
want without thinking
gives me pleasure.
Amy sometimes says she'll die at 37.
She was born on Friday the 13th
but she radiates luck like a wishbone.
Better to be under the snow,
the big moon
magnolia
thinking of friends
and contradiction.
And my left shoulder was warm
phone warm in my left hand
and warm light vapid
and breathing.
But what will happen to us?

What will happen to the snow
what will happen to everyone else?
Everyone lost, and the playground,
and the law for how it all scatters?

Snow rose to our cheeks and we spat it
felt it breaching and hurting our teeth.
We've been indignant and hurt
sailing through worlds
and the dirt.
The snow rose to our ears,
and we listened for movement and water.
We were too easily flattered, extreme,
even one reader felt miracle,
miraculous,
so rare I couldn't sequitur
and I couldn't non-sequitur neither.

But your grammar is so splendid I surrender.

Tell the others how elaborate the detail,
tell the special,
tell the tender,
tell the snow and the playground and babies.
Is it contradiction moves the snow?
Where's the grit?
And I thought I heard horses
And I thought I was silent
and the street quiet
and I always wanted to be quiet
and I always wanted to be language,
so great to be imperfect at night
and for spring to just collapse

and for the air around your heart
to fill with snow.

This is music for the Gods,
things and thing-language
and the snow that surrenders
when it touches your cheek.
Somewhere there's a glass maze
filling with sugar
where babies join the Union
and know what to do.

Can we find it?
What are people saying out in life?
Is someone peeling an orange?
Are the horses all nuzzled asleep?

I was hypnotized entirely,
falling down a cadence frozen blue.

And are you eating?
I was eating snow.

And I said to the snow,
don't leave me.

A little wire, a paperclip,
my instruments.

Snow with dirt all over it.

Fresh world arching to receive us.

ROSA

Solemn
pollen
fluttered
and disbanded
by the wind
come sudden
through the trees
world
rapid
and arranged
or just composed
by all you brilliant
sets of fabric
all you language
failing detail
I was spitting
French cherry stones
into the fire
I was spitting
French cherry stones
into the trees
adore me
adore my vulgar emblems
rust and static
futile contours
or the contours
of futility
you could take
away the F
like a motivational
speaker

speaking havoc
to the relics
of the century
while the evidence
of sunset
just crashes
through the trees
spraying pink
on lime
reminds me
of the mosque
on the corner
of our street
in blue and green
from glass and tiles
and men all
standing
side by side
but now I'm blending
rapid world
come sudden
and arranged
if I send out signals
for the poets in my sleep
then what's the difference
what's the sleep
sleep anagrams
that's how I used to
split infinitives
now it's like
this
rearrange the inside
composition

depression's just a dip
it's like a system
you prepare for
just some muted joy avoiding
all my absent ailments
all my detail faulty
blush embarrass syntax
it's the airwaves
woodsmoke coming home
I wasn't ready
home a jaybird
with a blue wing
turning turning
spent my language money
on a locksmith
write a thousand poems like this
and retire
show your bruises
to the ruins
withdrawn endorsement
bandaged front door
inner mirror
poems do this
fuck your life up
walk you from the porch
into the orchard
teach you that the
purest form of prosody
is gossip
hyperbole the cousin
of devotion
anaesthetics in the wild
blue yonder I can think them

frontwards and the other
and the gesture
light behaving
like a convoy
blue above the wing
and white beneath it
all the neutral tones
alone and flanked
all you sleeping tones
who trust it
stuffed with gliding light
and fortune fortune
have to press it with your mouth
in soft and glassy
imperfections
stuck I'm sticking
with my story
there are hymns
to incandescence
we forget
and paper legs
don't always follow
paper head
and breathless breathless
still had access
to the accents
of my childhood
words for food and home
and stillness clipping
at the break
for damaged houses-
thread to daytime thread
and heavy treading

on the grass
the heavy feeling
still won't lift
entirely thinking
of the difference
between 5 and 6 a.m.
the boys of summer
stealing cars
feeling precious
avant-garde
and dead I always
think of rural life
as vague as family
knowledge
all the secret
countries
you belong to
all the buried
feelings
all the drinking
on a bridge
and throwing bottles
at the road
beside the river
spitting French
cherry stones
into the stream
a dog
running wild
and sunset crashing
permanent resistance
to the distant and the near
whatever comes between

the dreaming volatile
surprise me
set the desk on fire
in stupid tribute
by a tree
select a signal
and a person
to receive it
could be catch you
could be cash
it could be study up
and do it on behalf
of someone you both knew
who could have done with knowing
what else is there
but to run in all
directions to the sea
and will it spill you always
like a compass
in a white room
like a dog
returning
list for memory's
urgent modulation
when we came
inside the house
and the radio applauded
it was constant
and the airwaves
swept up pieces
for the premise
and the promised
orange blossom

for the toasting of the poets
who dissolve into the crowd
like Mao said
if we were fishing
we were sunk
we were hook short line
and sinker
neon tetra
trench
European perch
Atlantic salmon
common mackerel
dogfish
common skate
and bait for catching
everything you need
and everybody else
felt something ending
before the vote on Brexit
we were drinking
at the art show
and a student
pouring wine
just threw a tonne of ice
right out the window
and when the fascists
marched through Whitehall
back in May
there wasn't any kind of crowd
to slip back into
just the Trotskyists
whose twisting trust
is good for nothing

what's the deal
what's the
deal
what's the ruffled talent
singing when it sings
to all the plaintive plaintiffs
slick different and drastic
what's the treatment
say you speak from wounded
starting like a flinch
a dog returning
say you speak
from pristine districts
say you see
a burnt-out building
struck and silent
all the airborne metal
flattened panic
wrapped in plastic
listen up
the opposite of urgency is safety
but safety's always urgent
like a moving contradiction
like a dog
running circles
depressed and last to sleep
eating blossom
and defensive
thud thud
surrounds your heart
surrounds your lungs
and makes your eyeballs wet
with blinking

flung head back
to face the facing sky
star blind and broke
choked up with suspect skill
but I'm an amateur
missing my cue
every time I hear a nightingale
I think I hear a blackbird
it's shameful
all you daytime poets
all you one-time poets
stillness
incandescent
and resistant
Creeley said the plan
is the body
but I think
the body is the body
the plan is the plan
and there are many bodies
but I love it all the same
I love the certain grammar
green light shimmer
light green sweetness
you discover
nothing beats this
language spoken
is a circle first of all
or maybe oval
local to the speaker
today it's cool
a little rain
metallic clouds

who's keeping count
the dog asleep
the pollen high
alone in someone
else's house
you keep on seeing
movement
in the corner
of your eye
but this is just
the nervous feeling
of the eye the house belongs to
this is what it means
to be a guest
crunch crunch
goes the person
waking up
at 5 or 6 a.m.
thinking of the music
and the paintings
of the mid-to-late
last century
smell of roses
woodsmoke
lime flower
and rain
my cosmology
versus
my body
the total crush of living
under finance
the constant threat of war
is sign the war

already started
think of fear of
mental breakdown
formal stories
talk stories
for steering and thinking
and the dog's teeth clicking
gunshots to the East
and West and engine
starting
Sunday hunting
desperate fragments
stitched together
what that looks like
is a fabric
and we've seen it
and the window
where it issues
and just because
it's narrative
doesn't mean
it's equals
think of bending light
and light's bent pattern
absurd and gradual
in abandon
this trick's easy
because the words all
know each other's names
aerial breakfast cereal
dealing early fearless
gentle hearing inside
jealous kicking lesson

making open perfect
quiet resets tasted
under violent water
x-ray yearly zero
and you find it
and it feels good
and this is called aesthetics
teaching vowels and treasure
at a standstill
what to do and how to do it
and I realise writing like this
is an insult
to a sector
of the dead
but since I'm
still young
since I'm young still
I'd like to keep it loose
and let the language
fuck around
eight miles of sky
and sky defended
ragged world
and vague
as the numbers in love
at the margins serrated
names and movement
twisted into order
every time I leave the city
feel it different
isn't theory
it's praxis
asthmatic

used to think
repetition was death
the same as dying
now I realise
it's impossible
impossible
impossible granular
while the dog eats a moth
the breeze outside is moving
East to West
like the sun
I throw some dust up
to prove it
and the dog looks unimpressed
the dog looks hungry
so I feed her
half a kilo
of raw meat
thinking of my body
and if the plan is
in the body
it would be
mainly in the bones
fuck DNA
but paper bones
don't always follow
paper plans
or hollow planes
or revamp
feasible
like paper amnesia
first thing I remember's
interdiction

toy truck on the threshold
of the flats
I couldn't have
entirely Oedipal
as it should be
pushed around by dreams
what I wanted
was to sing life
speak it
type it out and see
if it was true
so test it
like the dog at sunset
barking at the graveyard
lavender maximum
maximum lilac
I'm lying
what I wanted
was for everyone I know
to line the streets
whatever street it is
it doesn't matter
shit I lived in Wales
in the eighties
line the fields
but I don't know
what starts
I'm calling storms
I'm hearing harps
I'm seeing poets
work the land
it's dangerous thinking
traction

to the cultural
attaché
but harvest time was wild
continual dusk and sunset
dogs all running laps
but what will happen
what will
happen
last two years
suspended stupid vortex
I could bang my head against
but my skull just passes through it
and I whistle through my ears
when I'm in public
but the Welsh dogs of the 1980s
they can't hear me
and the English dogs
of later decades
don't respond
and there are no dogs
in Scotland
and in Ireland
the running dogs
are running in the North
and I was spitting
French cherry stones
into the sink
I was spitting
French cherry stones
out of the window
I was thinking
it's just me
and the dog

and the milk pail
the breeze and the birds
and the GDP
the rooster
the chainsaw
the predatory loans
the border
the wasps
and the flies
fascists in Hungary
fascists in Rome
fascists all over the map
rabbits in the fields
outrunning hunters
punctured by sunset
the branches
the leaves
and the bark
waiting for the day
to slip unnoticed
for the dark
to stick around
and keep us busy
my poem
my poets
my notebook
and my car

ON POINT

Hölderlin says night and distress
makes us strong. I keep getting it
wrong, mistaking waking up
for one of living's great achievements.
If life is big I'm small inside it,
the song increases
                        and all the creatures
keeping night a better secret
thrown together, quit faking death
quit making silence stand for art
how it trips off the tongue
                    and falls down the stairs
summer through the transfer
of heart to heart to heart
you and the light and the air

WET HECK

Joy and surprise my staple diet
feeling forwards like a dog
I wanted to do this
and I could hear your English voices
go sometimes the ceilings, sometimes the floors
                                                            oh my dudes
who with arcane fibre would believe it
city lawns seen from above
everyone's brother
covered by insurance
                                    everyone's tactic
obscure like the heart thinking honeycomb
vanilla this week more expensive than silver
the horizon menaced by sugar
oh my dudes
                        August exhausted my attitude
help me to do this
                        the theory of the epic in the lyric
psychoanalysis
            not even clouds a kind of halo
sinking and soaking my feet
and I was watching it happen
standing in my worn-out high-tops
three months and the seams split
                                                            a kind of rip-off
a waste of everyone's time
I was watching it happen
everyone furious, everyone old
and wildfires
                              turning the orange sky orange

three-fifths of the plough on a rooftop in the breeze
lifting my t-shirt
against the green sky
          and for an hour the building looks so good
nothing sounds right
lulled into midnight, oh my dudes
I saw whole families gang up on sea life
children holding lobsters and chanting in triumph
the men waving away in expensive shoes
                                        and also the women
in expensive shoes also
seven white shirts drying on the line
                         and we were leaning in the wind
and the wind went through our pockets
tell my parents I owe them some money
can protect them
from the night and three types of cruelty
          everyone living and everyone dead
get in here
I have something to tell you

SLINGSHOT

Wake up universe fabric shaking dust
certain in a beige hotel you must
keep your life exactly as it is
                                        still sleeping to my right
you're breathing not that deep air
just the normal inside air
                    we were breathing last night
                              and I was learning to write
without playing hostage
                                        or is it captive to my life
since I'm here all the time
          the audience warm and touching my arm
and everyone sharing their passwords.

Send me some words I can end this with:

          sweet grapefruit
          golden forest
          normal hold

HALF KING GOLDEN EXTERIOR

Maybe every generation
needs its own Catullus
what the fuck
hand me my sugar-free 7up

Caesar cries all the time
Caesar cries all the time

and I'm no-one's paper horse
peeling apples in the carefree
economy.

Call him luck
Call him luck

the internet saps
passenger passage me now.

Be true to the art of your time:

two years ahead
two years behind

all anyone needs is a brilliant line

DIAL P. FOR PAINTING

for Charline von Heyl

Acrylic singing the pictures
peach crystal and suspicious
struck by lightning
making plans to deface
the grave of Ezra Pound
in the dawn-light
with our fingers double-crossed
and the air superstitious
and the great fake lagoons
too yellow for schemes
the weird light humid and futile.

Do you believe in salvation?
Yes sometimes.

I get paint on my clothes on my own.

A giant black phone
and a giant hand pointing
and the pictures all singing us back.

THROUGHOUT BUILDING

Don't be sad and not know it
unhappy, turmeric, said a group of strangers
in my dream. A boat called Jupiter Clipper
not in my dream but all around it
a song full of facts for July.
                    We were walking in South London
telling everyone everyone's secrets
                    on a boat called Jupiter Heatwave
reckless relating the gestures of trust
like a French poet, chaotic adolescence
we were saving each other's lives
playing names for no-one and nothing
on a boat called Jupiter Nothing
love the skeleton skeleton first

EVERYBODY'S BIRTHDAY

for TW and JD

Sometimes climb inside the piano
& speak to my hired mourners
waking up at the end of sleep
if my mouth is dry I can wet it
from an island, from wide Tennessee
put the wires between your teeth & hum
throw some salt on my shoulder
the name of this song is ice & soda
to the corners I leave my decorum
& we take up our podium places
every year I come here
                    to scream at the wildlife
for my own impossible encouragement
I thank each of you in turn

TEMPLE ASSOCIATION

For JL

Grass on the opposite roof
and beyond that the sky
that comes between us is gone

and anyone in California
could be raising a flag
what kind of flag?

South Coast yellow cranes
still in imitation afternoon
holding your pink book

to my pink ear singing
like a big blank cheque
catching thought in the middle

of its own obsolescence
glints wild lime
is the scent to dip your hands in

spoke Orpheus in his sleep
to his chickens
who love whatever love brings

mainly wild samphire and vaguely
like forgetting a language
plastic and the fabric next to plastic

HOME RADIO

For PG

But you tune the ghosts for everybody else,
roses on the table by the window
and even though the birds are quiet it's Sunday
and maybe you're quiet, listening out
in a different landscape, different weather.
We call this structure September,
and I'll stay in this tempo as long as I have to.
The roses are pink and the filament hums
and the shadows in the room look good.
Clean roses and ghosts on the radio.
I should clean the room but I won't.
Work greying my hair at the temples. Life too,
the era of ghosts, the epoch, the classics,
                    the poem.
And someone is bouncing a ball, someone
is stacking the dishes, someone is healthy
and someone is sick, and a dog barks
in the blue day, the kind you want for later fire
to remember. I love it when the door is open
and I can hear the world. The toothache light.
The water out of reach. Speech is just a thing
the dead do to remember what we said.
You said: *the blossom is stronger than us*
years ago, tired and vivid Cambridge spring.
I know this song. I know this toothache.
Love tends to the embers.
I believe this all the time.

ALMOND MILK

Now I'm all depth
and the people around me
crowd in,
turn to people inside
alive on a diet
of liquids and solids
a duet a duet
a duet a duet
a duet a duet
I don't crawl for.

Inner life.

Bundle up the air
to break your fall.
Deep is just another word
for surface
and everything's great
everything's great
everything's great
except the poison
and what the poison
represents.

The missing square.
The indecision.
The urge to vanish.

How do horses do it.
How do camels.

AUDIT AND ASSURANCE

After A.Z.

Turn up the stupid escape routes
        default broadcast I wake up to
                jaw wired shut
                        inhaling airborne metal
a little vocal movement
                the morning score
                                        yelp yelp
                                and all the questions
all the talk of adoration
                        what's all this talking?
Devotion, loyalty, touching.
                                        Where are you?
        Tinnitus, whistling, static.
Zero thought, zero action
                        zero love, zero landscape
now even trembling starts to falter
                vocal movement
                                comfort cooling
and you were shaking in the distance
                                        glazing over
all that twee shit
                                another season
waiting for the poets to remember how to do it
                all the stunts
                                        the old moves
                        chiselling blossom
from expensive trees
                                bruised, miserable, alive
and the water out of reach
                and even falling with poise

even thinking of impact
and a scene so big
it could hold everyone's hands
hold everyone hostage
to tender resignations
to fortune here I am
and what I'm here for is stalling
and the movement of history
I don't know.
There was this other life you used to go to
all of these hymns
to provisional life
and who the green light flatters
with elegant footwork
trees that give up
secrets to sleep through
and the floorplan
the floorplan of the body
curves and stops
witness to spring
for the 32nd time
it doesn't matter
but I mean it
falling in a courtyard
and the men outside the centre
threaded to the railings
where the air pulls us together
and everyone's hands
in the shape of a pocket
never finished
it was day
but now it's night
but it was day
and footsteps in the hallway

already there
whoever gets home first
stupid, frightened
and who the voices were was government
business
community leaders
hired thugs
minor royals
YouTube floating heads
teenage libertarians and ancient racists
on a video link too big to ignore.

And who was I?
And where have you been?
And what's all this talking, and everything spilling?
And the defectors, where were they and who?

And then so undone you undo.

You push down and across and you loop,
stuck sticking to the letter,
stuck to writing by hand
stuck to writing by hand, he said.

You win.

And on the outside of the inside
the borders closing tighter
and the blossom white

chewed up and spat out

spitting and whistling and spitting.

ROTE CODA

What we want is surface come back
champion clusters, what we want
is sober April scripts consensus
hands free from the national average
the avant-garde and what we did with it
the numbers, the shades, the late fees
the whole gang stupid in replacement
all that, what we endless rest on
                                        and all the body talk
and everyone's sore unbalanced throat
and not knowing and knowing that too
and not wanting to know

                                                        pages of elegant foothold

ANGEL TYRE UNIT

What the day does up to no-one
through a glass door does it go
to where you've got to get to
whole streets still sleeping and the people
hours ago, heavy sky and the sky even louder
soft power, I hate the summer when it starts
and when it ends I tell my friends this
sure enough & restless over
gather damage to the limit overflow
and if you fake transparent who will save you
song not exactly clouds for writing down with
bad grace junk science and mortal resting my voice
close to mute and nearly midnight are you ready
I can't remember who says what to who

NARRATIVE ATOMS

Asleep above the modem and the fields,
perfect like that, but the fleeting pattern
feels like you don't need the I do too.
Blue sky future textile, choose your poet.
Confuse the air with exile lying down,
surrounded by a crowd of tired tourists
clouds like ribs, and a student of ethics
declaring his love for the format.
The only thing I really care about
is the end of the 20th Century, what it was
I walked in on, and who I have to see
to get a refund. Hold my ticket.
I came here to be quiet and be changed,
corner of people all raising my heart.
I stayed through ostrich hours,
wrote *production* for *protection*, tried it out
and gave away the measure in my speeches.
But stay cool in your calcium deficit,
rehearsing your perfect excuses.
I need the name of daybreak on the table,
shaped into effigy, mute and unsuitable,
and the sky completely embarrassing.
I pressed my face against the screen

and you did too, and those were moves
that we would never have to recreate,
hazards beaten up, slow and slow-clumsy
swaying in time to our inscrutable music.
And you know and you know and you know
the voice contingent is a pulped thing
a jealous thing, all credit where credit is due.

Stop thinking with your mouth full.

I always hated show and tell.

JUNE BAD ADVICE

The ninth consecutive
year of the rat.

Someone told me.

I saw four foxes.

Someone told me.

Wild mint and sunlight on metal,
        had to go inside and tend internal
                        phoneme tender
with my back to the forest
        real hands clapping real body
                mock planet
like to talk about scale
        green immature green blanket
                speckled with credit, speckled with gain
someone told me
                just to watch the country disappear
        and the brains with a toe in the discourse
grapefruit juice and lemonade
                slate luminous grey
                                reaching for it
        wild irritate skin
                        light method
didn't get the memo got the rumour
                and my body still only a checklist

check who’s listening
        rough public brushed the surface
                                        sheer and glassy
and there are other bodies
        doing body things
                                        someone told me
it’s the season for praising
                                        praise everything

WAIFS AND STRAYS
for IC

'Eat the garbage you like.'

'Translate your victories.'

& the earth just swallows you
up.

The dry rhythm is different,
white clover and poppy
I can't explain it.

Complete pine trees
if you let them win
the birds come free
completely plastic.

John said and I believe him
he can tell underground
where the train is
by changes in the air.

Like vertical trapdoors
could have been the title
but it wasn't.
                                        And I headache.

Spring begins in the mountains,
never reaches the sea.

And there's a big red fence
on Gray's Inn Road

perfect metal syllables

the sunset at standstill

sparkling bullshit

Something hurts,
it is my hand.

Sounds like me and I don't like it.

What begins now.

Who begins it.

POEM

And aren't you tired,   of everything folded
into true and regular feelings, and the word
for what I'm looking for, more edges serrated
less less it's okay, where's my gold
neck-brace, where's my gold peacock
buried in the yard
          and the boys with embroidered shovels
shove it and the damp ground back
the joke is you're still here
                    using your real boots in hard decay
and I cover my name tag
go to sleep for ten years
the great poem about suffering
the great poem about not suffering
throw everything away / keep everything

HISTORY LESSONS

1.

Closed envelopes
chrysanthemums
ski slopes

the most boring film
I ever saw
the biggest star

the costume drama
printed and spoken

green apparatus

hydrangeas
my money
the institute

2.

tread delicate epic
epic quality epic

hand over hand over absence

3.

big culture red buttons

come animal floating

grey a little orange
in the bricks

4.

three cool texts
in invisible ink
means everything

diagram pink
on multiple platforms

nowhere safe
and nowhere ruined

almond moonlight
dozens of thumbs
the national culture

you look at X
X looks at you

give up and chew

5.

to sidestep capital
get up and clap

me and my kneejerk
cousin Jupiter normal

write what you cough
on-off on-off

6.

vertical windows
ambient sunlight
auto-cathect

the person had edges

the person

7.

phonebooks mulched

the one-sided art

with its movements

8.

police flood the streets
testing the budget
spring after spring

dress up your parents
as prophets

9.

and you little drum
what gossip to the numbers

pushing record
in the smiling snow

green beans and lettuce

ceremony triplets

inglorious georgic

10.

dry mouth
arm calendar

projectors

watching the street
class struggle

a light bulb

the sleep that goes bang

bust all your acts
all at once

WINTER JOURNEY

Everything you could is what you did
however fucked up
wasn't always what we wanted
even slightly
slightly knows
what it says
and how it ends
about a thing
to identify
with any going thing
and anything returning
to the body
snowing in the vein
whoever saw him
dead in winter at the edge
could tell you something
however fucked up nothing
more nothing left behind

today the birds are sharp

the birds are starving

SOLO POST ILIASSA S.

a thousand
pine trees

ugh

twenty
turbines

multiplied
by zero

waking up
drinking coffee
eating walnuts

ugh

I hate the dirty air
I love the sky

ugh

today
the world is flimsy

the word
is horse

is jawbone & eyelid

mutiny chainsaw

green plume
blue stream

'I saw a bonfire'

and clouds
like grey cream

well anyone can learn
to write a sentence

ugh

the day
with its drawn-out mouth

and sense of occasion

hurts my eyes

one of my bodies

stayed out too late

YAWN AND STRETCH

The ears leave in singles and in pairs,
flee the country
move from coast to coast
take up different habits,
put on different clothes,
blameless golden children
older now and happy
with holes in our sides
each of us living
neither alive,
we felt like guarantees
and so did you,
flat-footed and exact
cheap shots
high jumps at the prospect
a giant hallway decked with statues
and a voice at every window:

You will never be entirely still
not the same but something other
other lessons, other people
other loss—

This is the wrong
house.
The walls are shorter
than the steps,
it's always
cold
the roof leaks
milk

the lights go back
into the table
you burn your hand,
you break your leg,
you make
attachments
come apart
but happy
or at least enough
inside the bedroom
or the kitchen
or the street.

Put an exclamation
mark up on my headstone.

No thank you.

The day is open
and I have to go—

have to go to golden apples
with our pockets falling out
lips all pressed to solar panels
knuckles in the grass
and all the trees in Essex
torn in half.

The heart is a method under protest.

Keep your apparatus
to yourself.

17/3

Right now narcissi, gentle heat
bare feet in the morning
sharp green of the world

fresh sheets:
the airlines at standstill
and everything ready

and whoever's off the hook
in the middle of the woods
or on a private island

what's left is to take it
the landscape and everything else

to turn away and keep turning

bad distance:

whatever burns off
another life in the chest

4/4

Yap yap yap. What's left in my
head hurts, waving goodbye
to who we've been seeing, but intenser:
closed spaces of dogs and birds, April,
and all of it clasped, a violet glass
mid-century tokens. If language is object
and object broken open
who will outlive it before I do?

The grey plastic gutter can't decide
if it's blue, can't make up my mind
on the structure of trust:
high notes — animals — shields.
                                                  I'm just
isn't anything: I'm more
and more now, now the quiet
breaks ranks, gives itself up
                              to the current according
pushes you around pushes you around
wild version of day
                                stop beginning

14/4

What else is there to do?
Get up and study whatever's outside the window?
Continue the careful and patient study of whichever
book can hold my attention?
Our problems are everyone's
the universal hinge to catch your finger,
index or middle, it matters.
        Green shoots every day reject the economic
or that's how I think it, out of reach,
and the man sleeping under blossom a whole week
you treat it as fixtures, biting your tongue.
Walk out and the smell is of firewood.
Who is that?
                A kind of house and relation,
an arrangement.
                        There are models.
The formal gardens are transparent.
All the species of grass laid out to begin with,
bordered by wild and improbable flowers.
                                        No borders.
Everything has to move upwards.
Is that true?
                Who will do the heavy lifting
and the dozen other gestures
                                of tenderness,
whatever we asked for,
                        strong violets, gold,
the same questions
on hold:

Now everything moves all at once, into place,
snaps shut or uncurls, in language as it's talked
and *by who*, staple diets
                                        and the synapse rhythm
of spring.
                    Wasps happy in the blossom
keep circling the flat. I imply everything:
I see it as my job, put the surface back together
on everything.

The green corner unfolds.

A slice of apple,
a glass of water,
the state above our heads
behind our backs—

Somebody loves it.

I don't want to be saved.

18/4

Say the voices over walls, no walls,
but the fearful lovers, lime and air
the whistles let you laugh along
                                        sometimes keep you
in the awake part of life
overcast and punctured by the blue
                                                            at least my head
tells me when I turn it if it's hurting.

If it sounds true, if the walls are voices,
little ribs, and the person that breathes them
I could feel it in the morning pressing in:

the standing up and nothing to stand up to,
impatient hydration, gulped down before you cut
the faux-naïve imperatives and give yourself
a plateau to look down from.

                                                                        The air
in the live room, floating to keep up.

Lighting a candle
                                                            for the merely, for the new

How superstitious are the days
you barely live through.

19/4

Being lied to all the time is nothing new
but the position of the dead
                    apocalypse ice pops
still ringing in my ears
and here
          the dogs are going on, you get it,
doubled up with jealous backstrokes
      the nest and types of nesting
tight and sutured arches —
      I go in here and make a tunnel
the body is five tunnels
          each hand five tunnels also:
the lungs are lakes the heart's
a mountain this is stupid
                    but transformation's
still the central pleasure of our art.

I saw a blackbird choking on a worm,
a kind of troubled joy and now
               a little patina of guilt
ripens in the daylight
               waiting for parts
of the world to wake up in

      You can't get by on attributions.

The world of appearances,
coming to an end.

VENTOLIN

What they like is direct sunlight
song like glue
and how much things
cost if you want them
to stay still
and understand
defeat this time less euphoric
the disaster too diffuse
to just step into
racing to wake up
before the market
admire the morning air
and wolf it down,
watch them coughing up
holding history by the hand
with one hand
acute and unacknowledged
and with the other hand touching
my face.

Did you hear the one about
the epidemic?

Or the one about the epidemic
and the state?

I heard the one about
the epidemic
a kind of ache
the same as always
lost to the weather and vague
to still want it like this
the parts of the language

you do mouth-to-mouth to
most of you,
and all the time
sticky on lookout
for the gist.

It never gets old.

The prisoners in Modena
and Brixton.
The prisoners at Rikers.
The debris,
the missing
and the message,
what the messengers leave
this time this year
this time this month
this time this week
catching the difference
you tell it to a friend
complete and unretrievable
you patent the question
and give it away.

It gets old,
cut bleeding on the knuckle
stuck
piling up rewrites
what you find on the floor
just falls in
to your lap
like the head of a lover
floating downstream
you spring the day back faultless

break off the brocade
and taste of salt
and aloe vera
taste of salt
and aloe vera
taste of salt
and aloe vera
and alcohol.

Lyric poetry and sobriety.

It's *okay*.

I wouldn't always recommend it.

But it's *okay*.

It took years
it took forever
it took all day
and now it's done
keeping vigil
at the end
of the weird 2010s
spent a decade off my legs
and necking aspirin
while the sun
played aspirin
to the sky
said someone you don't know
in some other blunt decade
also thinking
of defeat
and have I been here
before,

did we meet somewhere once
did I say something terrible
and brilliant
the glory in shame
the memory of sweat
and who is it
déjà vu
will belong to?

The thing is you get older.
Your friends die.
You lose your sense of humour.
You move away.
And they also
come back
weathered surface
rocky outcrop
tie a ribbon
to the one
you want to cut down
tie a ribbon
to the one
you want to leave.

We were outside the British Museum
as unhappy
as it's possible
to be
we were drinking lime and soda
changing places in the world
what we wanted was the total break
but not like that
and not like this
hard to give a fuck about Etruscans

day colour
of pigeons
more gloomy
than blueish
keeping vigil's what I said
to the damage
and fuck a Virgil
and all the filled-in wish fulfilment
of camaraderie
and camaraderie's paranoid afterparty
who heard a rumour of voting
and a rumour of death
and a rumour of choosing
every time you check the news
you lose a life
and who the life belongs to
on the island sinking into floorboards
more than what we asked for less
or less than nothing less than that
locked in song for chewed-up evening
the mildest winter I remember
getting whiplash
had to learn it
had to sit through
a thousand odes to debt and business
a thousand more to inattention
ill-advised attempts at imitation
fawning under ruthless supervision
tasked with brilliance
in the fairest of the seasons
and the season's fairest failures
to transform.

Spring——
hand me my airhorn.
Hand me the phonebook.
Point
to the beautiful world :
you smell like sleep
and nothing else
getting fainter all the time
what passes for midnight
moon clipped on the left
dark blue and familiar
windows open
where I live
in retribution
was the shadow
for my friend
all broken up
before you
split
slipped off
drew a line
between the dying
I tried to tell you.

And now the light is dirty
the light
is dirty now
and now you turn a corner
in your head
and in the street
counting days lost to sickness
days lost to strikes
backwards from ten
and miss the target